HOW TO SELL ON ETSY FOR BEGINNERS

A detailed guide on how to make money on Etsy(Tested and Trusted)

LEWIS MADISON

Table Of Contents

A SUCCESS STORY TO MOTIVATE YOU

In a bustling city, nestled between towering skyscrapers and busy streets, lived Lily, a creative soul with a knack for turning dreams into reality. With a passion for crafting unique jewelry pieces, Lily found herself drawn to the enchanting world of Etsy.

Lily's journey on Etsy began with a small collection of handcrafted earrings that captured the essence of nature's beauty. Each piece she carefully designed seemed to tell a story of its own, and she poured her heart into every intricate detail. She knew she had something special, something that could resonate with people across the globe.

But success wasn't instant. Lily faced challenges and setbacks, from perfecting her craft to finding the right market. Yet, her determination was unyielding. Late nights turned into early mornings as she researched, experimented, and refined her techniques. Slowly but surely, Lily's creations began to shine in the crowded marketplace.

Her breakthrough came when a popular lifestyle blogger stumbled upon Lily's Etsy shop and fell in love with her jewelry. The blogger featured Lily's pieces in a post that quickly went viral. Suddenly, orders flooded in from all corners of the world, and Lily's little workspace transformed into a bustling creative haven.

Lily understood the power of customer experience. She meticulously packaged each order, adding a personal touch that made customers feel cherished. The word spread like wildfire, not just about her exquisite jewelry, but also about the care she put into every aspect of her business.

With her newfound success, Lily didn't rest on her laurels. She invested her profits back into growing her selection of goods. Her shop became a haven not just for jewelry enthusiasts, but for those seeking one-of-a-kind gifts that spoke volumes.

Collaborations with other artisans and designers followed, creating a synergy that elevated her shop's uniqueness.

As the years went by, Lily's Etsy shop grew beyond her wildest dreams. She had transformed her passion into a thriving business that provided financial stability and a sense of purpose. Lily's story became an inspiration, showing that with dedication, creativity, and an unwavering commitment to excellence, Etsy could be a gateway to not just success, but to a life illuminated by the radiant glow of one's own creativity.

And so, in the heart of the city's vibrant rhythm, Lily's Etsy journey blossomed into a symphony of artistic expression and entrepreneurial triumph, leaving an indelible mark on the world and a proof of the amazing opportunities available to individuals who dare to imagine and make.

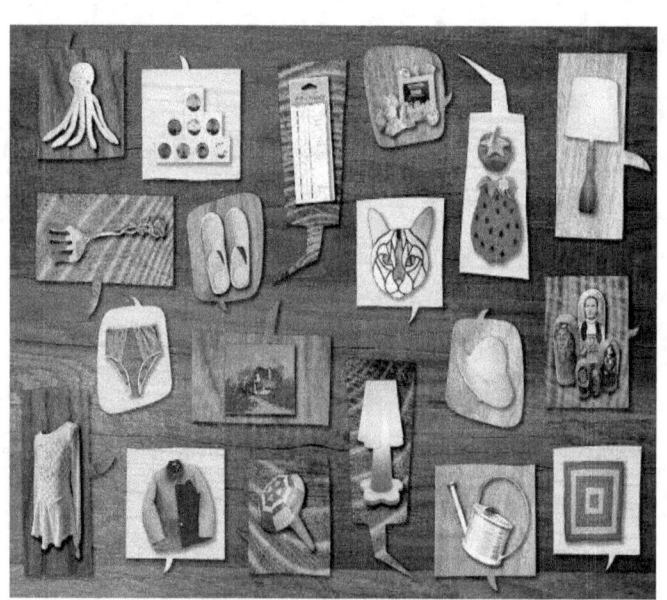

PART I: Introduction to Etsy Selling

Welcome to the exciting world of Etsy, a global marketplace where creativity meets commerce, and artisans like you have the opportunity to showcase their unique creations to a worldwide audience. Whether you're a seasoned craftsman or a budding entrepreneur, Etsy offers a dynamic platform to share your passion, connect with customers who appreciate the value of handmade and vintage items, and build a successful business that aligns with your creative vision.

Understanding the Unique Appeal of Etsy:

Etsy stands out in the e-commerce landscape due to its focus on creativity, originality, and community. Unlike traditional online marketplaces, Etsy provides a haven for artisans, designers, and vintage enthusiasts to sell their goods, offering buyers a refreshing alternative to mass-produced items. This emphasis on individuality has fostered a sense of authenticity that resonates with consumers seeking items imbued with personal stories and artistic flair.

Pros and Cons of Etsy Selling:

Before embarking on your Etsy journey, it's essential to consider the advantages and challenges that come with selling on this platform.

Pros:

Global Reach: Etsy's international presence means your creations can be discovered by buyers from all around the world.

Niche Audience: Etsy's user base consists of individuals actively seeking handmade, vintage, and unique items, which aligns well with your creative offerings.

Community and Networking: Etsy's vibrant community provides a space to connect with fellow sellers, gain insights, and exchange valuable experiences.

Ease of Use: Setting up an Etsy shop requires minimal technical expertise, making it accessible for newcomers to e-commerce.

Customization: You have the freedom to personalize your shop's branding, layout, and policies to reflect your artistic identity.

Cons:

Competition: With the platform's popularity, you'll encounter competition from other skilled sellers within your niche.

Fees: Etsy charges listing fees, transaction fees, and optional advertising fees. You must incorporate these expenses into your pricing plan.

Algorithmic Changes: Etsy's search algorithm evolves, affecting the visibility of your listings. Staying updated on SEO techniques is essential.

Time and Effort: Running an Etsy shop requires consistent effort in terms of product creation, customer service, and marketing.

Limited Control: While you can personalize your shop to some extent, you're still working within Etsy's framework.

Setting the Stage for Success:

Establishing your presence on Etsy begins with creating a captivating shop profile and crafting a unique brand identity. This includes selecting a shop name that resonates with your offerings and target audience, designing an eye-catching banner and logo that reflect your style, and crafting a compelling shop announcement that tells the story behind your creations.

In this journey, remember that Etsy is not just a marketplace; it's a canvas for your creativity to flourish, a platform to connect with fellow artisans and buyers who appreciate your craft, and an opportunity to turn your passion into a profitable venture. By mastering the art of Etsy selling, you'll unlock a world of potential where your creations can inspire, resonate, and make a meaningful impact

Understanding the Unique Selling Points of Etsy

Etsy, the renowned online marketplace, has carved a distinctive niche for itself in the world of e-commerce. It stands as a beacon for artists, artisans, vintage enthusiasts, and creative entrepreneurs seeking to connect with a global audience that values authenticity, uniqueness, and human touch in their purchases. By comprehending the unique selling points (USPs) of Etsy, you gain insight into why this platform has become a go-to destination for both sellers and buyers who appreciate the finer aspects of craftsmanship.

Handcrafted and Unique Offerings:
At the heart of Etsy's allure is its dedication to craftsmanship. Unlike conventional e-commerce platforms that predominantly offer mass-produced goods, Etsy places artisans and creators at the forefront. Sellers on Etsy provide products that are thoughtfully designed, meticulously crafted, and

often imbued with personal stories. This focus on the artisanal journey and the intimate connection between creator and creation resonates deeply with buyers who seek items with character, charm, and a touch of the artist's spirit.

Vintage Treasures and Unearthed Gems:

Etsy's unique blend of new and vintage offerings presents a treasure trove for vintage aficionados and collectors. Vintage sellers on Etsy curate items that evoke nostalgia, tell stories of the past, and bring timeless elegance to the modern world. The platform's commitment to maintaining the authenticity of vintage pieces ensures that buyers can acquire pieces of history while supporting a sustainable shopping ethos.

Supportive Creative Community:

Etsy is not merely a marketplace; it's a thriving community of like-minded individuals who share a passion for creativity and entrepreneurship. Sellers can engage with fellow artisans, exchange insights, seek advice, and build connections that transcend geographical boundaries. This sense of camaraderie fosters an environment where learning and growth are embraced, making Etsy a platform that nurtures talents and encourages collaboration.

Personalized Shopping Experience:

Etsy's user interface is designed to facilitate personalized discovery. Its intuitive search algorithm considers factors such as product relevance, shop popularity, and buyer preferences. As a result, buyers are presented with products that align closely with their interests, leading to a more fulfilling shopping experience.

Connection to the Creator:

Etsy bridges the gap between buyer and seller, offering a direct channel of communication. This enables buyers to engage with creators, ask questions, request customizations, and establish a personal connection that's often absent in traditional retail environments. This sense of direct interaction adds value to the purchase and creates a more meaningful transaction.

Celebrating Creativity and Originality:

Etsy's dedication to celebrating individuality empowers creators to showcase their unique visions. This focus on originality and self-expression encourages sellers to experiment with designs, techniques, and materials, resulting in a diverse range of products that cater to a wide array of tastes and preferences.

Ethical and Sustainable Shopping:

Etsy aligns with the growing demand for ethical and sustainable shopping. The platform's emphasis on handmade and vintage items promotes eco-conscious consumption, allowing buyers to make purchases that have a reduced environmental impact compared to mass-produced alternatives.

In summary, Etsy's unique selling points rest upon its celebration of craftsmanship, its vibrant community, its personalized shopping experience, and its dedication to authenticity and creativity. By understanding these distinctive qualities, you'll be well-equipped to navigate the Etsy marketplace, make informed selling decisions, and resonate with buyers who share your appreciation for the extraordinary. As you embark on your Etsy journey, remember that you're not just selling products; you're offering pieces of artistry and stories waiting to be discovered by an audience that values the beauty of the handmade and the allure of the unique.

Pros and Cons of the Etsy Marketplace

Embarking on the journey of selling your unique creations on Etsy opens up a world of opportunities and considerations. As with any venture, there are both advantages and challenges associated with participating in the Etsy marketplace. Understanding these pros and cons will help you make informed decisions as you navigate this creative ecommerce platform.

Pros:

Global Exposure and Reach: Etsy boasts a vast and diverse user base, offering you the chance to showcase your products to a worldwide audience.

This global exposure enables you to connect with buyers from different cultures and regions.

Niche-Focused Audience: Etsy's community is composed of individuals who actively seek handmade, vintage, and distinctive items. This focused audience is more likely to appreciate the value of your craft, increasing the potential for sales.

Ease of Setup: Creating an Etsy shop requires minimal technical know-how. The platform provides user-friendly tools that guide you through the process of setting up your shop, listing products, and customizing your profile.

Customization Options: Etsy allows you to tailor your shop's branding, policies, and layout to reflect your unique style and identity. This customization helps establish a cohesive and memorable brand image.

Networking and Community: The Etsy community is a vibrant space where artisans and entrepreneurs interact, share insights, and offer support. Engaging with this community can provide valuable advice and connections.

Cons:

Increased Competition: The popularity of Etsy means that you'll face competition from numerous skilled sellers within your niche. Standing out requires a combination of creativity, marketing, and high-quality products.

Fees: Etsy charges listing fees, transaction fees, and optional advertising fees. While these fees contribute to the platform's services, they impact your profit margins and pricing strategy.

Algorithmic Changes: Etsy's search algorithm evolves, affecting the visibility of your listings. Staying up-to-date with search engine optimization (SEO) techniques is vital to maintaining your shop's discoverability.

Time and Effort: Running a successful Etsy shop demands consistent effort. This includes creating and updating product listings, handling customer inquiries, processing orders, and managing shipping.

Limited Control: While you can customize your shop to some extent, you're still working within Etsy's framework. This may limit your ability to implement certain design elements or functionalities.

Dependency on Platform: Your shop's success is tied to Etsy's policies and changes. Relying solely on one platform can lead to vulnerability if there are unexpected policy shifts or disruptions.

In conclusion, the Etsy marketplace offers a myriad of advantages for creative entrepreneurs seeking to showcase their crafts. However, it's important to be mindful of the challenges that come with the territory. By leveraging the pros and proactively addressing the cons, you can strategically position your Etsy shop for success. Careful planning, continuous learning, and a commitment to delivering quality products and excellent customer service will contribute to your journey as an Etsy seller. As you navigate this dynamic platform, embracing both the benefits and potential pitfalls will empower you to make the most of your creative endeavor.

PART II:Getting Started on Etsy:Establishing Your Creative Business

Embarking on the journey of selling your creative products on Etsy is an exciting endeavor that requires thoughtful planning and strategic execution. This guide will provide you with a comprehensive overview of the essential steps to get started on Etsy, helping you set up a strong foundation for your creative business.

Creating Your Etsy Account:

The first step on your Etsy journey is to create an account. Visit Etsy's website and click on the "Sell on Etsy" option to begin the process. You'll be guided through a series of prompts to set up your shop name, select your preferred language and currency, and agree to Etsy's policies.

Choosing Your Shop Name and Branding:

Your shop name is a critical aspect of your brand identity. Select a name that reflects your products and resonates with your target audience. Keep it memorable, unique, and relevant. Once you've chosen your name, consider creating a captivating logo or banner that represents your style and captures the essence of your creations.

Crafting Your Shop Announcement and About Page:

Your shop announcement and About page are your opportunities to introduce yourself to potential customers. Craft a shop announcement that provides a brief overview of your offerings and sets the tone for your brand. The About page allows you to share your story, inspiration, and creative journey, adding a personal touch to your shop.

Uploading a Profile Picture and Banner:

Enhance your shop's visual appeal by uploading a profile picture and banner that align with your brand. Your profile picture can be a headshot or a logo that represents you as the face behind your creations. The banner is a larger image that can showcase your products or your artistic style.

Defining Your Niche and Product Range:

Identify the niche you want to focus on within the vast creative landscape. Define the types of products you'll offer, whether they're handmade crafts, vintage items, or supplies. Narrowing down your niche helps you target a specific audience and stand out amidst the competition.

Listing Your Products:

Listing your products is a pivotal step in setting up your Etsy shop. Each listing should feature clear, high-quality images of your products, compelling titles, detailed descriptions, and accurate pricing. Be transparent about dimensions, materials, and customization options if applicable.

Pricing Your Products:

Pricing your products requires careful consideration of factors such as material costs, labor, overhead, and market value. Strive to strike a balance between your company's profitability and your customer's capacity to afford it.

Setting ShoStrivep Policies:

Define your shop policies to establish guidelines for shipping, returns, exchanges, and customer interactions. Clear and concise policies build trust and ensure a seamless shopping experience for your customers.

Payment and Shipping Settings:

Set up your payment preferences, selecting from options like Etsy Payments and PayPal. Configure your shipping settings, specifying regions you ship to and estimating delivery times. Accurate shipping information is essential for customer satisfaction.

Preview and Launch Your Shop:

Before launching your shop, preview your listings and profile to ensure everything is in order. Review your shop announcement, product listings, policies, and branding elements. Once you're confident, hit the "Open Your Shop" button to officially launch.

By following these steps, you'll lay a strong foundation for your Etsy shop, positioning yourself for success in the competitive world of online selling. Remember that success on Etsy requires dedication, continuous improvement, and a genuine passion for your craft. As you embark on this journey, embrace the opportunity to connect with a global community of like-minded creatives and eager buyers who appreciate the beauty of handmade, vintage, and unique items

Setting Up Your Shop: Profile and Branding

Establishing a compelling shop profile and cohesive branding is the cornerstone of your success on Etsy. Your shop's visual identity and the story you convey play a pivotal role in attracting customers and building trust. Here's a detailed guide to help you create an inviting and memorable shop presence.

Crafting a Striking Profile:

Profile Picture:Choose a profile picture that showcases your personality or your brand logo. It's the first visual impression customers have of you, so ensure it's clear and professional.

Shop Name:Select a shop name that captures your niche, style, or personality. Make it memorable and relevant to your offerings.

*Shop Announcement:*Craft a welcoming and engaging shop announcement. Use this space to greet customers, introduce your brand briefly, and convey your shop's unique selling points.

*About Section:*Use the About section to share your story. Explain your passion, journey, and what sets you apart. This personal touch fosters a connection with customers.

Designing Your Banner and Logo:

Banner: Create a visually appealing banner that represents your shop's vibe. It should evoke your brand's essence and captivate visitors' attention.

Logo: If applicable, design a logo that embodies your brand identity. A well-designed logo enhances brand recognition and professionalism.

Color Palette: Establish a consistent color palette that aligns with your brand's aesthetics. This palette should be reflected in your banner, logo, and shop elements.

Typography: Choose a legible font for your shop's text elements. Consistency in typography contributes to a cohesive visual experience.

Establishing Brand Consistency:

Product Photography:Maintain consistency in your product photography style. Use similar lighting, backgrounds, and angles to create a unified product presentation.

Listing Descriptions: Craft product descriptions that align with your brand's tone. Consistent language and style across listings enhance your brand's image.

Shop Policies: Infuse your brand voice into your shop policies. Ensure they reflect your commitment to quality and customer satisfaction.

Communication: Respond to customer inquiries and messages with a consistent tone and professionalism. Every interaction is an opportunity to reinforce your brand's identity.

By investing time in crafting an inviting shop profile and establishing cohesive branding, you're creating a shop that customers can trust and resonate with. Remember, your profile and branding elements tell the story of your creations and connect with buyers on a personal level. A well-defined brand presence sets the stage for a memorable shopping experience that keeps customers returning for more.

Navigating Etsy's Interface and Tools: A Comprehensive Guide

Etsy's user-friendly interface and tools are designed to empower sellers with the resources they need to manage their shops efficiently and connect with buyers effectively. Here's a detailed overview to help you navigate Etsy's interface and leverage its tools for a successful selling experience.

Shop Dashboard:
Upon logging in, you'll land on your shop dashboard. This central hub provides an overview of your shop's performance, including sales, traffic, and recent activities. Use this space to monitor your shop's health and track key metrics.

Listings Manager:
Access the Listings Manager to view, edit, or create new listings. You can easily update product details, images, and pricing. Utilize tags and attributes to

optimize searchability and improve your listings' visibility.

Shop Manager:

The Shop Manager is your command center for all things related to your shop. It includes sections such as Orders, Listings, Finances, and Marketing. This comprehensive tool enables you to efficiently manage orders, track revenue, and implement marketing strategies.

Conversations:

The Conversations tab allows you to communicate directly with buyers. Timely and professional responses enhance customer satisfaction and build trust. Utilize this tool to address inquiries, provide assistance, and manage customer interactions.

Etsy Payments:

Etsy Payments is a secure and convenient way to handle transactions. It allows you to accept a variety of payment methods, providing a seamless checkout experience for buyers. Keep your payment settings updated for smooth processing.

Shipping:

Etsy's Shipping tool streamlines the process of managing shipping options, costs, and delivery times. Define your shipping profiles, specify regions you ship to, and offer tracking information to buyers for peace of mind.

Promoted Listings:

Etsy offers a Promoted Listings feature to boost the visibility of your products. Set a budget, select listings to promote, and optimize your campaigns for maximum impact. Regularly analyze the performance of your promoted listings to refine your strategy.

Stats and Analytics:

Etsy's Stats and Analytics provide valuable insights into your shop's performance. Keep track of important statistics like views, favorites, and conversion rates. Use this data to refine your listings, marketing efforts, and overall business strategy.

Shop Policies and Updates:

Keep your shop policies up to date to provide transparency and clarity to customers. The Shop Updates feature allows you to share news, promotions, and new product launches with your followers.

Etsy Community:

Engage with Etsy's community of sellers through the Forums and Teams. These platforms offer opportunities to ask questions, share experiences, and learn from fellow entrepreneurs.

Mobile App:

Etsy's mobile app enables you to manage your shop on the go. Stay connected with customers, respond to messages, and track orders wherever you are.

By familiarizing yourself with Etsy's intuitive interface and leveraging its powerful tools, you'll be equipped to manage your shop efficiently, make informed decisions, and provide an exceptional shopping experience for your customers. Regularly explore updates and new features to stay ahead in the dynamic world of online selling. Remember, Etsy's interface and tools are designed to support your journey as a successful creative entrepreneur.

PART III:Product Creation and Optimization

In the world of Etsy, the heart of your success lies in the quality and appeal of your products. Crafting captivating items that resonate with your target audience and optimizing their presentation for maximum impact is a key element in establishing a thriving shop. This chapter delves into the art of product creation and optimization, guiding you through the process of creating remarkable offerings that stand out in a competitive marketplace.

Defining Your Creative Vision:

Before embarking on product creation, define your creative vision. Consider the aesthetic, style, and themes that encapsulate your brand. Your products should reflect your unique perspective, setting the foundation for a coherent and distinctive product line.

Ideation and Conceptualization:

Brainstorm product ideas that align with your creative vision and cater to your target audience's preferences. Research current trends and gather inspiration from various sources, such as nature, art, and culture. Sketch and outline concepts to bring your ideas to life.

Material Selection:

Choose high-quality materials that complement your design. Whether it's fabrics, metals, wood, or any other medium, the materials you select contribute to the overall value and durability of your products.

Skillful Craftsmanship:

Craft each item with meticulous attention to detail. Whether it's intricate stitching, precise engraving, or seamless assembly, the craftsmanship you invest in your creations elevates their perceived worth and authenticity.

Unique Design Elements:

Infuse your products with unique design elements that set them apart. Consider incorporating personalized touches, innovative features, or unexpected color combinations that capture the essence of your creative brand.

Pricing Strategy:

Establish a pricing strategy that is competitive and reflects the value of your items. Factor in material costs, labor, overhead, and desired profit margins. Balancing affordability for buyers with profitability for your business is key.

Creating Compelling Product Listings:

Listings are the digital storefronts of your products. Craft engaging product titles that succinctly convey the essence of your offerings. Write detailed and informative descriptions that highlight key features, dimensions, and materials.

Showcasing through Imagery:

High-quality imagery is crucial in portraying the true beauty of your products. Capture multiple angles, utilize natural lighting, and ensure clear focus to provide an accurate representation. Include lifestyle shots to help buyers envision how your products can enhance their lives.

Optimizing SEO for Visibility:

Implement effective search engine optimization (SEO) techniques to enhance your products' visibility within Etsy's search results. Conduct keyword research to identify relevant terms buyers are likely to use when searching for products like yours.

Encouraging Engagement:

Incorporate engaging storytelling within your product descriptions. Describe the inspiration behind each item and the thought process that went into its creation. Sharing the story adds depth and personal connection to your offerings.

Embracing Iteration and Improvement:

Constantly seek ways to refine your products. Pay attention to customer feedback, monitor trends, and remain open to evolving your designs to meet changing preferences.

Mastering the art of product creation and optimization requires a blend of creativity, craftsmanship, and strategic thinking. By creating products that reflect your brand identity, resonate with your audience, and embody exceptional quality, you're well on your way to carving a niche for yourself in the vibrant world of Etsy. As you embark on this creative journey, remember that each product you create is an opportunity to tell a story, evoke emotion, and make an indelible impression on those who discover and appreciate your artistry.

Crafting Products with Market Appeal and Creating Engaging Product Listings

In the dynamic realm of Etsy, the heartbeat of your success lies in your ability to craft products that not only captivate your target audience but also resonate with the broader market. The magic happens when you intertwine your creative ingenuity with an acute understanding of market trends and consumer preferences. This chapter delves into the intricate art of crafting products that hold market appeal and the finesse of creating product listings that invite buyers to explore, engage, and purchase.

Crafting Products with Market Appeal:
Before your creative journey takes shape, it's essential to define your market appeal. This involves aligning your artistic vision with the

demands of your potential buyers. It's the delicate balance between your creative authenticity and the desires of your audience that sets the stage for products that not only shine but also sell.

Understanding Your Audience:
Take a deep dive into understanding the preferences, needs, and pain points of your target audience. What resonates with them? What aesthetics do they adore? This knowledge is the cornerstone of crafting products that hold a special place in their hearts.

Blending Creativity and Trends:
Infuse your artistic flair with current market trends. This fusion creates a synergy that results in products that are both unique and aligned with what's in demand. The key is to find that sweet spot where your creativity meets the desires of your audience.

Material Selection:
Your choice of materials not only affects the visual appeal but also the tactile experience of your products. Choose materials that resonate with your design vision and add value to your offerings.

Craftsmanship Excellence:
Meticulous craftsmanship is the backbone of products that stand out. Whether it's intricate embroidery, hand-carved details, or precision in assembly, the craftsmanship you invest in your creations communicates your dedication to quality.

Unveiling Unique Aspects:
What sets your creations apart from the rest? Integrate unique elements that tell a story. A

personalized engraving, an unexpected pop of color, or a distinct texture can elevate your products and make them memorable.

Pricing Deliberation:

Setting the right price is an art that involves striking a balance between perceived value and accessibility. Account for costs, labor, and profit margins while ensuring your pricing aligns with your target audience's expectations.

Creating Engaging Product Listings:

Once you've crafted products with market appeal, the next step is to create listings that showcase them in the best light. Your product listings are virtual shop windows that need to entice, educate, and encourage buyers to make a purchase.

Crafting Compelling Product Titles:

Your product titles should be concise yet descriptive, capturing the essence of what you're offering. Use keywords that your potential buyers are likely to search for while maintaining clarity.

Eloquence in Descriptions:

Craft detailed and informative descriptions that not only describe your products but also evoke emotion. Highlight key features, materials used, dimensions, and any unique aspects that make your creations special.

Visual Storytelling through Imagery:

High-quality images are non-negotiable. Invest time in capturing your products from various angles with attention to detail. Utilize natural light and consider including lifestyle shots to help buyers envision how your products fit into their lives.

SEO Magic:

Leverage the power of search engine optimization (SEO) to ensure your products appear in relevant search results. Research keywords related to your products and strategically incorporate them into your titles and descriptions.

Personal Touch:

Infuse your brand personality into your listings. Share the inspiration behind your creations, the story of your brand, or the process that goes into making each item. This personal touch connects you with potential buyers on a deeper level.

Clear Calls to Action:

Guide potential buyers on what to do next. From "Add to Cart" to "Shop Now," ensure your calls to action are clear and strategically placed to encourage engagement.

Ongoing Optimization:

Regularly assess the performance of your listings. Which ones are getting more views? Which ones are converting into sales? Use this data to refine your listings, from titles to descriptions, for optimal results.

In the dynamic landscape of Etsy, the alchemy of crafting products with market appeal and creating engaging product listings is a skill that evolves with experience and dedication. It's the harmony of artistic expression, market understanding, and effective communication that transforms your offerings into compelling works of art that beckon customers to explore and make a purchase. With each listing, you're not just showcasing products; you're extending an invitation for buyers to embark on a journey into your creative universe.

PART IV:Optimizing for Search and Discovery

In the bustling marketplace of Etsy, where millions of products vie for attention, the ability to optimize for search and discovery is a strategic advantage that can significantly impact your shop's visibility and success. This chapter delves into the intricate realm of search engine optimization (SEO) and strategic discoverability tactics, equipping you with the tools to ensure that your products rise to the top of search results and capture the attention of your target audience.

The Essence of Search and Discovery:
Search and discovery are the pathways through which buyers find your products amidst the vast sea of offerings. Effective optimization ensures that your creations are not only seen but also considered by potential customers.

Understanding Etsy's Search Algorithm:

Etsy's search algorithm is designed to deliver relevant results to users. It takes into account factors like relevancy, recency, and customer satisfaction to determine the ranking of products in search results.

Researching Keywords:

Keywords are the cornerstone of effective optimization. Research keywords that are relevant to your products and are frequently used by potential buyers in their searches.

Strategic Placement of Keywords:

Incorporate your researched keywords strategically in your product titles, descriptions, and tags. Ensure that they flow naturally and provide accurate context.

Crafting Compelling Titles:

Your product titles should be concise yet descriptive, including important keywords. A well-crafted title not only attracts attention but also helps your products rank higher in search results.

Detailed and Informative Descriptions:

Your product descriptions offer an opportunity to not only engage potential buyers but also include relevant keywords. Describe your products comprehensively, addressing key features, materials, and benefits.

Harnessing the Power of Tags:

Tags are an invaluable tool for expanding your products' discoverability. Include a mix of specific and broader tags that cover various aspects of your product.

Navigating Attributes and Variations:

Attributes and variations allow you to provide more specific details about your products, helping buyers find exactly what they're looking for.

Embracing Renewals and Updates:

Renewing your listings or making updates can impact their visibility. Use renewals strategically for products that need a boost in search rankings.

Monitoring and Analyzing Performance:

Regularly analyze the performance of your listings using Etsy's analytics tools. Identify which keywords are driving traffic and conversions, and refine your strategy accordingly.

Leveraging Off-Site Promotion:

Promote your products beyond Etsy through social media, blogs, and other platforms. Link back to your Etsy shop to drive traffic and improve your shop's overall visibility.

Customer Reviews and Engagement:

Positive customer reviews and engagement contribute to higher rankings. Provide exceptional customer service, encourage reviews, and foster a positive shopping experience.

Staying Updated with Algorithm Changes:

Etsy's algorithm evolves over time. Stay informed about any changes and adapt your optimization strategy to remain effective.

Optimizing for search and discovery is both an art and a science. It requires a deep understanding of your target audience, meticulous keyword research, and strategic placement of those keywords throughout your listings. By mastering the intricacies of Etsy's search algorithm and continually refining your optimization tactics, you're positioning your products to not only be found but also to thrive in a competitive marketplace.

Remember, each optimization effort is a step towards ensuring that your products are precisely where they belong—front and center in the eyes of eager buyers seeking the unique offerings you have to offer.

Demystifying Etsy's Search Algorithm and Strategies for Effective Keyword Placement

Demystifying Etsy's Search Algorithm:
Etsy's search algorithm is the digital gatekeeper that determines how products are presented to potential buyers. While the exact formula remains a secret, understanding its core components sheds light on effective strategies for increasing your products' visibility.

Relevance:The algorithm assesses how well your product matches a buyer's search. Aligning your keywords with customer intent is crucial.

Customer Satisfaction: Positive reviews, fast shipping, and excellent customer service contribute to higher search rankings.

Recency: Freshness matters. Recently listed or updated items often enjoy a boost in search results.

Strategies for Effective Keyword Placement:

Precise Product Titles: Craft concise, descriptive titles that include essential keywords. Think like a buyer and consider phrases they might use.

Contextual Descriptions: In your product descriptions, provide context and detail. Integrate keywords naturally while offering value to potential buyers.

Strategic Tags: Tags are direct keywords that amplify your products' discoverability. Mix specific and broad tags to reach various search queries.

Attributes and Variations: Use attributes and variations wisely. Incorporate keywords while providing options for customization.

Consistency is Key: Maintain keyword consistency across titles, descriptions, tags, and attributes. A unified approach strengthens your products' relevance.

Buyer-Centric Language: Use terms and phrases that resonate with your target audience. Reflect how buyers search for products.

Trends Awareness: Stay updated on market trends. Incorporate trending keywords to ride the wave of popular searches.

Avoid Overloading: While keywords are crucial, avoid stuffing your content. Keep readability and clarity intact.

Analyze and Adapt: Regularly review performance data through Etsy's analytics. Adjust your strategy based on which keywords are driving results.

External Promotion: Extend your reach beyond Etsy. Incorporate keywords in external promotions to enhance your online presence.

In the dynamic Etsy ecosystem, mastering the synergy of effective keyword placement and understanding the algorithm is your ticket to increasing visibility and attracting buyers. By aligning your listings with what customers are looking for, you optimize your products for search and discovery, ensuring they're not only seen but also sought after. Remember, each keyword strategically placed is a step towards unlocking the potential of Etsy's search algorithm in propelling your products to the forefront of buyers' searches.

PART V:Customer Engagement and Satisfaction

In the realm of Etsy, where creativity and commerce converge, the journey doesn't end at a sale—it thrives through customer engagement and satisfaction. This chapter delves into the crucial art of building strong relationships with your buyers, ensuring their experience goes beyond a transaction and transforms into a lasting connection that breeds loyalty and word-of-mouth promotion.

The Significance of Customer Engagement:
Customer engagement is the lifeblood of your Etsy journey. It goes beyond the sale, encompassing interactions before, during, and after a purchase. Engaging customers fosters trust, encourages loyalty, and ultimately drives the growth of your brand.

Crafting an Inviting Shop Atmosphere:
Your shop's atmosphere sets the stage for engagement. Craft a welcoming and organized

shop layout, and ensure your shop policies and FAQs are easily accessible. Transparency breeds trust.

Responsive and Timely Communication:

Promptly respond to inquiries, messages, and concerns. Effective communication demonstrates your commitment to customer satisfaction and leaves a positive impression.

Personalization and Customization:

Offer personalized touches whenever possible. Whether it's a handwritten thank-you note or a tailored recommendation, personalization showcases your genuine care.

Exceptional Customer Service:

Go above and beyond to meet customer needs. Address concerns promptly and professionally. Handling issues gracefully can turn an unsatisfied customer into a loyal advocate.

Post-Purchase Engagement:

Engage customers after the sale by expressing gratitude and seeking feedback. This interaction not only encourages repeat business but also opens avenues for improvement.

Leveraging Packaging and Presentation:

Elevate the unboxing experience. Thoughtfully package products to delight customers upon delivery. Include branded materials or small surprises to leave a lasting impression.

Nurturing Loyalty:

Reward repeat customers with exclusive offers, discounts, or early access to new products. Loyalty programs show appreciation and encourage ongoing engagement.

Harnessing Social Media:

Make use of social media to interact with clients outside of Etsy. Share behind-the-scenes glimpses, product launches, and customer stories to foster a sense of community.

Seeking and Implementing Feedback:

Customer feedback is a goldmine of insights. Use reviews and suggestions to refine your products, enhance customer experience, and showcase your commitment to growth.

Handling Challenges Gracefully:

Mishaps are opportunities for growth. Handle negative reviews or challenges with grace, addressing concerns publicly and demonstrating your dedication to resolution.

Measuring Customer Satisfaction:

Regularly assess customer satisfaction through reviews, surveys, and post-purchase communications. Analyzing trends helps you adapt and refine your engagement strategies.

Continuous Improvement:

Customer engagement is an evolving process. Continuously seek ways to enhance the customer experience, whether through enhanced communication, more personalized interactions, or improved services.

In the vibrant world of Etsy, customer engagement and satisfaction aren't just boxes to tick; they're cornerstones of your brand's success. Every interaction, from the first inquiry to the post-purchase follow-up, is an opportunity to create meaningful connections, build trust, and leave an indelible mark on your customers' minds and hearts. By prioritizing engagement and ensuring satisfaction, you're not only driving your Etsy venture forward but also creating a community of loyal patrons who champion your creations and share their positive experience

Establishing Clear Shop Policies and Effective Communication and Customer Service

In the bustling marketplace of Etsy, establishing clear shop policies and mastering effective communication and customer service are pivotal for cultivating a trustworthy and customer-centric brand. This chapter delves into the art of creating transparent shop policies, fostering open lines of communication, and providing top-notch customer service to ensure a seamless and satisfying experience for both you and your buyers.

Crafting Clear Shop Policies:

Transparency and clarity in your shop policies build trust and set expectations for your buyers. Clearly outline essential details, such as shipping times, returns, exchanges, and payment methods.

Shipping and Handling Information:

Specify your shipping methods, estimated delivery times, and any additional charges. Setting accurate expectations reduces confusion and enhances customer satisfaction.

Returns and Exchanges Guidelines:

Clearly define your policies for returns and exchanges. Address scenarios such as damaged items or incorrect orders. Easy-to-follow instructions ensure a smooth process for both you and your customers.

Payment Policies:

Outline accepted payment methods, currency, and any applicable taxes or fees. Transparent payment policies contribute to a positive purchasing experience.

Effective Communication:

Open lines of communication are the foundation of strong customer relationships. Respond promptly to inquiries, address concerns, and maintain professionalism in all interactions.

Timely Responses:

Promptly address customer inquiries and messages. Timely responses show your commitment to customer satisfaction and build trust.

Customization and Personalization:

If you offer customized products, maintain clear communication throughout the process. Ensure customers are informed about timelines, design options, and any associated costs.

Courtesy and Professionalism:

Communicate with courtesy and professionalism at all times. A positive interaction leaves a lasting impression and encourages repeat business.

Handling Customer Issues:

Challenges may arise, but how you handle them matters most. Address customer concerns empathetically and offer solutions that prioritize their satisfaction.

Providing Top-Notch Customer Service:

Going the extra mile distinguishes exceptional customer service. Offer assistance, answer questions, and resolve issues swiftly and amicably.

Resolving Disputes:

In cases of disputes or misunderstandings, approach resolutions calmly and rationally. Put finding compromises that work for all parties first.

Feedback and Continuous Improvement:

Customer feedback is invaluable. Encourage reviews and use constructive feedback to refine your policies, communication strategies, and overall service.

Multichannel Communication:

Engage with customers through various channels, such as Etsy messages, email, and social media. Be accessible and responsive across platforms.

Training and Empowering Staff:

If you have employees or team members, ensure they are well-versed in your communication and customer service strategies. Consistency is key.

Learning from Customer Interactions:

Each interaction is a learning opportunity. Identify trends, patterns, and areas for improvement based on customer interactions.

Establishing clear shop policies and excelling in effective communication and customer service set the stage for a positive shopping experience. By creating transparency, being accessible, and prioritizing customer satisfaction, you're not only building a loyal customer base but also enhancing your shop's reputation as a reliable and customer-focused brand. Remember, the interactions you have with your customers are the building blocks of lasting relationships, repeat business, and enthusiastic recommendations that can propel your Etsy venture to new heights.

PART VI:Strategic Marketing Strategies

In the ever-evolving landscape of Etsy, where creativity meets commerce, mastering strategic marketing is the linchpin that propels your products from obscurity to prominence. This chapter delves into the intricacies of effective marketing strategies, showcasing the potency of leveraging social media for widespread exposure, executing impactful promotions, and adeptly managing comprehensive marketing campaigns that amplify your shop's reach and resonate with your target audience.

The Art of Strategic Marketing:

At its core, strategic marketing is the art of crafting a seamless bridge between your creations and potential buyers. It involves understanding your customers' needs, crafting compelling narratives, and adopting methods that align with your brand identity.

The Power of Social Media Exposure:

Social media isn't just a platform—it's a dynamic stage where your products can shine. Choose platforms that match the aesthetics of your brand and appeal to your target market. Use captivating visuals, engaging captions, and hashtags strategically to broaden your reach.

Crafting a Strong Social Media Presence:

Create social media profiles that mirror the essence of your Etsy shop. Consistency in visual aesthetics, tone, and messaging reinforces your brand identity and fosters recognition among your audience.

Engaging Content Creation:

Content is king in the realm of social media. Develop a content strategy that blends product highlights with behind-the-scenes glimpses, customer stories, and user-generated content. Captivate your audience's attention with diverse and relatable content.

Strategic Posting Schedule:

Timing is everything. Craft a posting schedule that takes into account your target audience's online activity patterns. Posting consistently during peak engagement hours maximizes your content's visibility.

Running Effective Promotions:

Promotions are potent tools to spark buying interest. Offer discounts, bundle deals, or exclusive perks strategically. Be clear about the promotion's duration and terms to encourage conversions.

Navigating Seasonal and Event-Based Promotions:

Align your promotions with relevant holidays, seasons, and events. Tailoring your offers to resonate with these moments taps into the emotional triggers of buyers, enhancing your chances of capturing their attention.

Crafting Compelling Campaigns:

Campaigns are immersive stories that captivate your audience. Develop a central theme that aligns with your brand's essence. Infuse consistency in visuals, messaging, and storytelling to create a memorable impact.

Multichannel Campaign Integration:

Extend the reach of your campaigns by integrating them across multiple channels. From your Etsy shop to your website and social media, cohesive messaging amplifies your campaign's resonance.

Leveraging Paid Advertising:

Paid advertising can yield substantial results. Invest in platforms like Etsy Ads or social media ads, targeting the right audience with precision. Monitor performance metrics to optimize your investment.

Data-Driven Insights:

Regularly analyze campaign data to gain insights into your audience's behavior. Metrics like click-through rates, conversion rates, and engagement levels provide valuable feedback for refining your strategies.

Monitoring and Managing Campaigns:

During your campaigns, stay vigilant. Monitor comments, messages, and engagement levels. Respond promptly and make real-time adjustments based on the audience's reactions.

Balancing Long-Term and Short-Term Strategies:

While promotions offer immediate impact, don't neglect the significance of long-term strategies. Building a consistent brand presence and nurturing customer loyalty is equally vital.

Collaborative Campaigns:

Collaborations with influencers or fellow Etsy sellers can amplify your reach. Partner with individuals whose values align with your brand for mutually beneficial exposure.

Strategic marketing strategies encompass a dynamic blend of techniques that go beyond mere promotion. By strategically harnessing social media, orchestrating compelling promotions, and orchestrating meticulous campaigns, you're curating an unforgettable brand narrative that resonates deeply with your audience. Always remember that marketing is a continuous voyage, and the strategies you employ today lay the foundation for your shop's enduring growth and impact tomorrow.

Running Promotions and Managing Marketing Campaigns

In the dynamic world of Etsy, running effective promotions and orchestrating successful marketing campaigns can be the key to propelling your shop's visibility, attracting new customers, and boosting sales. This chapter delves into the intricate strategies of running promotions and managing comprehensive marketing campaigns that resonate with your target audience and elevate your brand's presence.

The Power of Promotions and Campaigns:
Promotions and campaigns are strategic tools to create excitement, drive engagement, and entice buyers. Well-executed promotions can generate a surge in sales, while thoughtfully managed campaigns foster brand loyalty and awareness.

Crafting Compelling Promotions:
Effective promotions captivate attention and drive conversions. Consider various types of promotions,

such as discounts, free shipping, bundle deals, or exclusive offers.

Defining Promotion Objectives:

Start by outlining clear objectives for your promotions. Are you aiming to boost sales, clear inventory, attract new customers, or reward loyal ones? Your objectives shape your strategy.

Setting Clear Terms and Timing:

Clearly communicate the terms of your promotion, including start and end dates, eligibility criteria, and any applicable codes or requirements. Transparency builds trust.

Leveraging Seasonal and Event Opportunities:

Tie promotions to relevant holidays, seasons, or events. Capitalize on moments when buyer intent is high to maximize the impact of your offers.

Promotion Communication:

Promote your offers through multiple channels—your Etsy shop, social media, email newsletters, and website. Consistent messaging ensures that your audience is aware of the promotion.

Monitoring Performance:

Track the performance of your promotions. Measure metrics such as increased sales, website traffic, and engagement to gauge effectiveness.

Managing Marketing Campaigns:

Campaigns are holistic storytelling experiences that weave a narrative around your brand. Effective campaign management involves strategic planning, execution, and analysis.

Defining Campaign Goals:

Determine the goals of your campaign—whether it's to launch a new product line, highlight a collection, or raise awareness about your brand values.

Crafting a Central Theme:

Develop a central theme that aligns with your campaign's goals and resonates with your target audience. Your theme guides the visual and messaging components.

Multichannel Integration:

Extend your campaign across multiple platforms. Maintain a consistent brand presence by integrating the campaign's visuals and messaging into your Etsy shop, website, and social media.

Content Creation and Storytelling:

Create captivating content that tells a story. Share behind-the-scenes insights, customer testimonials, and product demonstrations to engage your audience.

Rollout Strategy:

Plan the phased rollout of your campaign elements, from teaser posts to the grand reveal. Building anticipation heightens excitement among your audience.

Monitoring Engagement and Adjusting:

During the campaign, monitor audience engagement and feedback. Be prepared to make real-time adjustments based on the response.

Post-Campaign Analysis:

After the campaign concludes, analyze its impact. Evaluate metrics like engagement rates, click-through rates, and conversions to gain insights for future campaigns.

Iterative Improvement:

Use insights from each campaign to refine your strategies. Experiment with different themes, messaging styles, and content formats to continually improve your campaign effectiveness.

Running promotions and managing marketing campaigns are dynamic endeavors that require meticulous planning, creativity, and adaptability. By crafting compelling promotions and weaving engaging narratives through campaigns, you're creating a multifaceted approach that not only resonates with your audience but also deepens their connection to your brand. Remember, each promotion and campaign is a brushstroke in the canvas of your shop's story, painting a vivid picture that draws customers in and keeps them engaged for the long haul.

PART VII: Beyond the Basics: Advanced Techniques

As you embark on the journey of mastering Etsy, delving into advanced techniques can elevate your shop's success to new heights. This chapter is your gateway to exploring sophisticated strategies and innovative approaches that go beyond the basics, enabling you to stand out in a competitive marketplace and carve a distinctive niche for your brand.

Refining Product Photography:

Advanced photography techniques can make your products shine even brighter. Experiment with creative lighting, angles, and compositions to capture attention and showcase intricate details.

A/B Testing for Optimization:

Harness the power of A/B testing to refine your product listings. Test different titles, descriptions, and images to identify which elements resonate best with your audience.

Segmented Marketing:

Tailor your marketing efforts by segmenting your audience. Create customized campaigns based on factors like purchase history, interests, or demographics for a more personalized approach.

Limited-Edition Releases:

Generate excitement by offering limited-edition products. The scarcity factor can drive urgency and exclusivity, enticing buyers to make a purchase.

Cross-Promotions with Complementary Shops:

Collaborate with fellow Etsy sellers whose products complement yours. Cross-promotions can introduce your brand to new audiences and create a mutually beneficial partnership.

Exclusive Subscriber Content:

Offer exclusive content or discounts to subscribers through an email newsletter. Building a loyal subscriber base can foster repeat business and build a community around your brand.

Interactive Live Streams and Q&A Sessions:

Engage with your audience in real-time through live streams and Q&A sessions. This interactive approach fosters a deeper connection and showcases the personality behind your brand.

Elevating Customer Unboxing Experience:

Think beyond packaging by creating an immersive unboxing experience. Add personalized notes, surprises, or branded materials to make the customer's opening moments memorable.

Customization and Personalization:

Advance beyond standard products by offering customization options. Let customers personalize colors, materials, or designs to create a unique product tailored to their preferences.

SEO Mastery:

Take your SEO expertise to the next level. Dive deep into keyword research, analyze competitor strategies, and continuously optimize your listings for peak visibility.

Innovative Product Launches:

Innovate your product launches by building anticipation through teaser campaigns, countdowns, or interactive sneak peeks that create buzz and excitement.

Sculpting a Signature Brand Voice:

Cultivate a distinctive brand voice that reflects your values and resonates with your audience. A consistent tone across all interactions builds a memorable brand identity.

Leveraging Data Analytics:

Harness advanced analytics tools to glean deeper insights into customer behavior, trends, and sales patterns. Data-driven decisions can refine your strategies for maximum impact.

International Expansion:

Explore international markets by offering worldwide shipping and tailoring your listings to different regions. This expansion opens doors to a global customer base.

Continuous Learning and Adaptation:

Etsy's landscape evolves, and so should your strategies. Stay updated with trends, algorithm changes, and industry developments to remain at the forefront of innovation.

Mastering advanced techniques requires dedication, experimentation, and an eagerness to explore uncharted territories. By pushing the boundaries and embracing innovation, you're positioning your shop as a beacon of excellence, capable of thriving in a competitive marketplace.

Remember, the advanced techniques you employ today are the stepping stones to the unparalleled success your Etsy venture can achieve tomorrow.

Enhancing Listings with Professional Photography

In the visually driven world of Etsy, where products are showcased through screens, the impact of photography cannot be overstated. High-quality and professionally executed product photography is the cornerstone of enticing potential customers and establishing a credible and appealing brand presence. This chapter delves into the art of enhancing your listings through professional photography, providing you with comprehensive insights to captivate your audience and drive conversions.

The Visual Language of Photography:

Photography is a universal language that communicates the essence of your products without words. It's your opportunity to convey craftsmanship, quality, and uniqueness that sets your offerings apart.

Investing in Professional Photography:

Consider professional photographers who specialize in product photography. Their expertise in lighting, composition, and editing can elevate your listings to a whole new level of attractiveness.

Showcasing Product Details:

Professional photography enables you to capture intricate details that may otherwise go unnoticed. Highlight textures, colors, patterns, and fine craftsmanship that tell the story of your products.

Creating Consistent Brand Aesthetics:

Create a unified visual look that captures the essence of your brand. Consistency in color schemes, backgrounds, and lighting across your listings enhances brand recognition and trust.

Choosing the Right Backgrounds:

Select backgrounds that complement your products and don't overshadow them. Neutral tones or minimalistic settings often work well, allowing your products to shine.

Mastering Lighting Techniques:

Lighting is the heartbeat of photography. Proper lighting enhances clarity, highlights features, and creates a captivating ambiance that draws viewers in.

Composition and Framing:

Try out several compositional strategies, such as the rule of thirds, leading lines, and symmetry. These techniques guide the viewer's gaze and create visually appealing arrangements.

Multiple Angles and Views:

Showcase your product from various angles and perspectives. Customers want a comprehensive understanding of what they're buying, and multiple views fulfill that need.

Lifestyle and Contextual Shots:

Incorporate lifestyle and contextual shots to demonstrate how your product fits into customers' lives. This approach helps buyers envision themselves using your offerings.

Image Editing and Retouching:

Professional editing enhances your images, removing distractions, adjusting colors, and optimizing exposure. Editing ensures your product's true essence is conveyed.

Maintaining Image Consistency:

Whether you have a few or many listings, strive for consistency in photography style. Uniformity enhances your shop's professionalism and fosters a cohesive brand identity.

Branding through Imagery:

Incorporate branding elements such as logos, labels, or watermarks into your images. Subtle branding reinforces your shop's identity in every customer interaction.

Mobile Optimization:

Consider mobile users when designing your images. Mobile shoppers form a significant portion of your audience, so ensure your images are clear and impactful on smaller screens.

Feedback and Iteration:

Seek feedback from peers or customers to refine your photography. Iterative improvement based on constructive criticism sharpens your photography skills over time.

Elevating your Etsy shop through professional photography is an investment that pays dividends. Your images become your shop's ambassadors, speaking volumes about your commitment to quality and professionalism. By capturing the essence of your products with finesse, you're creating a visual narrative that invites customers to explore, connect, and ultimately make a purchase. Remember, each well-crafted image is an invitation to experience the world of your products, making professional photography an indispensable tool in your journey toward Etsy success.

Harnessing Etsy Ads for Greater Visibility

In the bustling marketplace of Etsy, standing out from the crowd is a challenge every seller faces. Etsy Ads offers a strategic avenue to amplify your shop's visibility, reach a wider audience, and drive conversions. This chapter provides an in-depth exploration of how to effectively harness Etsy Ads to increase your shop's prominence and ultimately enhance your success.

Understanding Etsy Ads:

Etsy Ads is a powerful advertising tool designed to put your listings in front of potential buyers who are actively searching for products similar to yours. It uses a pay-per-click (PPC) business model, so you only pay when someone clicks on your advertisement.

Setting Clear Advertising Goals:

Before diving into Etsy Ads, define your goals. Are you looking to increase sales, boost visibility, or promote specific products? Clear goals guide your campaign strategy.

Keyword Research:

Keywords are the foundation of successful Etsy Ads campaigns. Research relevant keywords that align with your products and resonate with your target audience.

Creating Targeted Campaigns:

Etsy Ads allows you to create campaigns based on specific keywords or products. Tailor your campaigns to match your objectives, whether it's targeting broad search terms or honing in on niche keywords.

Setting Budgets and Bids:

Determine your daily budget and bid amounts. Etsy Ads provides recommendations, but consider your shop's financial capacity and campaign goals when setting these figures.

Crafting Compelling Ad Copy:

Write engaging ad titles and descriptions that entice users to click. Emphasize the special qualities, advantages, and worth of your product.

Optimizing Product Listings:

Before running ads, ensure your product listings are optimized. High-quality images, detailed descriptions, and accurate tags enhance the effectiveness of your campaigns.

Monitoring and Analyzing Performance:

Regularly monitor your Etsy Ads campaigns. Analyze metrics such as click-through rates (CTR), conversion rates, and return on ad spend (ROAS) to assess performance.

Adjusting Strategies:

Based on performance data, refine your campaigns. Pause underperforming keywords, increase bids on high-converting ones, and experiment with different ad variations.

Leveraging Ad Scheduling:

Use ad scheduling to display your ads at specific times of the day when your target audience is most active. This ensures optimal visibility and engagement.

Utilizing Retargeting:

Retargeting allows you to show ads to users who have previously interacted with your shop. It's a potent strategy to attract new clients.

Testing and Experimentation:

Don't shy away from experimentation. Test different ad variations, keywords, and strategies to identify what resonates most with your audience.

Balancing Organic and Paid Traffic:

Etsy Ads complements your organic efforts. Strive for a balance between paid and organic traffic to maintain a well-rounded approach to visibility.

Continual Learning and Optimization:

Etsy's advertising landscape evolves, so staying informed about new features and trends is crucial. Keep improving your campaigns to stay ahead.

Tracking and Reporting:

Etsy Ads provides valuable insights through its reporting tools. Monitor your campaigns' progress and adjust your strategies based on the data.

Harnessing Etsy Ads is a strategic maneuver that can significantly enhance your shop's visibility and potential for success. By leveraging the platform's targeting capabilities, data-driven insights, and flexible campaign structures, you're actively placing your products in front of the right audience at the right time. Remember, effective Etsy Ads campaigns are not static; they require continuous monitoring, adjustment, and a willingness to adapt to changing dynamics, ultimately helping you navigate the competitive Etsy landscape with finesse and achieve greater visibility and conversions.

PART VIII: Operational Efficiency and Growth

Operational efficiency is the backbone of sustainable growth in the world of Etsy. As your shop gains momentum, it's crucial to streamline processes, optimize resources, and embrace strategies that allow for consistent expansion. This chapter offers a comprehensive exploration of how to foster operational efficiency while setting the stage for long-term growth in your Etsy venture.

The Role of Operational Efficiency:
Operational efficiency involves maximizing output while minimizing input. It's about using resources effectively to streamline tasks, reduce costs, and enhance overall productivity.

Organized Inventory Management:
Efficient inventory management prevents overstocking or stockouts. Utilize inventory tracking tools to stay informed about product availability and ensure seamless order fulfillment.

Workflow Optimization:

Analyze your shop's workflow. Identify bottlenecks and areas where processes can be streamlined, automated, or better coordinated to save time and resources.

Effective Time Management:

Time is a valuable asset. Prioritize tasks, set schedules, and allocate time blocks for various activities to ensure maximum productivity and reduce time wastage.

Resource Allocation:

Allocate resources judiciously. Whether it's time, money, or manpower, channel resources towards activities that directly contribute to growth and customer satisfaction.

Outsourcing and Delegation:

As your shop grows, consider outsourcing non-core tasks or delegating responsibilities. This enables you to concentrate on your company's strategic components.

Strategic Partnerships:

Forge partnerships with suppliers, manufacturers, or service providers. Establishing reliable partnerships can streamline your supply chain and enhance overall efficiency.

Data-Driven Decision Making:

Leverage data analytics to make informed decisions. Insights from sales data, customer behavior, and market trends guide your strategies for growth.

Customer Relationship Management (CRM):

Implement a CRM system to manage customer interactions. A well-organized CRM helps in personalized communication, effective follow-ups, and enhanced customer satisfaction.

Scaling Responsibly:

Growth should be sustainable. Expand your offerings, marketing efforts, and operational capacity in alignment with your resources and market demand.

Continuous Learning and Innovation:

Stay updated with industry trends and innovations. Embrace new technologies and techniques that can optimize operations and contribute to growth.

Feedback and Adaptation:

Regularly gather feedback from customers, peers, and team members. Adapt your strategies based on feedback to continually refine and enhance operational efficiency.

Investing in Employee Development:

If you have a team, invest in their training and development. Skilled and motivated employees contribute to smoother operations and elevated customer experiences.

Risk Management and Contingency Planning:

Prepare for probable difficulties and anticipate them. Being prepared for disruptions safeguards your operations from unexpected setbacks.

Balancing Quality and Quantity:

As you scale, maintain the quality that defines your brand. Striking the right balance between quality and quantity ensures sustainable growth.

Measuring Success and KPIs:

Define key performance indicators (KPIs) that reflect your shop's growth objectives. Regularly measure and analyze these metrics to track your progress.

Operational efficiency is the compass that guides your Etsy venture toward sustainable growth. By optimizing processes, embracing innovation, and making informed decisions, you're not only ensuring smooth day-to-day operations but also paving the way for expansion and increased profitability. Remember, operational efficiency isn't a one-time endeavor; it's an ongoing commitment to refining your strategies, adapting to market dynamics, and fostering a culture of continuous improvement that fuels your journey toward success in the Etsy marketplace.

Mastering Time Management for Etsy Entrepreneurs

Time is a precious resource, especially for Etsy entrepreneurs juggling various tasks. Effective time management is essential for maintaining productivity and achieving business success. Here's a concise guide to help you make the most of your time:

Prioritize Tasks: Identify tasks that align with your goals and have the highest impact on your shop's growth. Focus on completing these tasks first.

Create a Schedule: Set a daily or weekly schedule that allocates specific time slots for different activities, including crafting, listing, marketing, and customer interactions.

Use Tools: Leverage tools like calendars, to-do lists, and productivity apps to stay organized and track your tasks.

Batch Similar Tasks: Group similar tasks together, such as responding to messages or creating product listings. This minimizes context-switching and improves efficiency.

Set Time Limits: Allocate a specific time frame for each task to prevent overcommitting and ensure you don't spend too much time on any one activity.

Minimize Distractions: Designate distraction-free periods for focused work. Silence notifications, close unnecessary tabs, and create a conducive workspace.

Delegate or Outsource: Consider outsourcing non-core tasks or hiring help for specific activities to free up your time for strategic responsibilities.

Learn to Say No: Don't overextend yourself. Politely decline tasks or opportunities that don't align with your priorities.

Take Breaks:Take regular breaks to refresh your thoughts and avoid burnout.   Short breaks can actually enhance overall productivity.

Reflect and Adjust: Review your time management techniques frequently.   Adjust your approach based on what works best for you and your business.

By mastering time management, you're enhancing your efficiency and creating space for strategic thinking and growth in your Etsy journey.

Using Analytics to Fine-Tune Your Approach

Analytics are a treasure trove of insights that can guide your Etsy journey toward success. Here's a succinct guide to help you harness the power of analytics:

Data-Driven Decisions: Leverage analytics to make informed decisions. Sales data, customer behavior, and website traffic patterns provide valuable insights.

Identify Trends: Spot trends in popular products, peak buying times, or seasonal shifts. Adjust your strategies to capitalize on these trends.

Track Conversion Rates: Monitor conversion rates to understand how effectively your shop turns visitors into buyers. Optimize listings and user experience accordingly.

Explore Traffic Sources: Analyze where your traffic comes from—direct, social media, Etsy search, etc. Focus on platforms driving the most engagement.

Monitor Click-Through Rates (CTR): Assess the effectiveness of your listings by tracking CTR. Higher CTR indicates compelling titles and images.

ROI on Advertising: Measure the return on investment (ROI) for your advertising efforts. Adjust campaigns based on which ones yield the best results.

Customer Insights: Gain a deeper understanding of your customers. Analyze demographics, preferences, and buying behavior to tailor your offerings.

Testing and Iteration: Use analytics to guide A/B testing. Experiment with different approaches and fine-tune based on what resonates with your audience.

*Spotting Underperforming Area*s: Identify low-performing listings, products, or strategies. Eliminate or revamp these areas to boost overall effectiveness

Regular Analysis: Make analyzing your shop's data a routine. Regular assessment helps you adapt to changing dynamics and refine your approach.

By embracing analytics, you're not just making decisions based on intuition—you're utilizing concrete data to steer your Etsy venture toward growth and success.

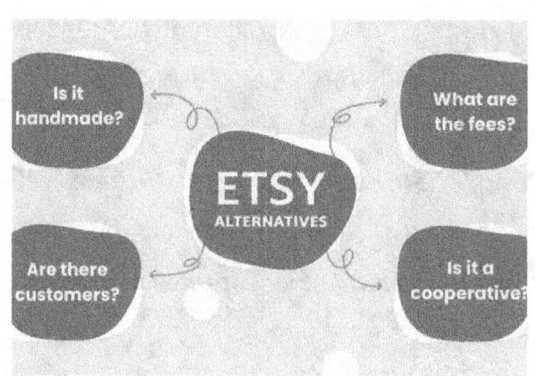

PART IX: Building a Strong Brand Presence: Crafting Your Etsy Identity

In the bustling realm of Etsy, where creativity converges with commerce, building a strong brand presence is paramount. Your brand identity is the heartbeat of your shop, shaping how customers perceive and connect with your offerings. This comprehensive guide explores the art of cultivating a distinctive brand presence that captivates your audience, fosters trust, and sets the stage for enduring success.

The Significance of Brand Presence:

Brand presence encompasses more than just a logo or color scheme. It's the amalgamation of your shop's values, personality, and the emotional connections you create with customers.

Defining Your Brand Identity:

Start by defining your brand's essence. What are your shop's values, mission, and unique selling proposition? These elements form the core of your identity.

Understanding Your Target Audience:

A strong brand resonates with its audience. Delve into your target customers' preferences, needs, and pain points to align your brand with their aspirations.

Visual Identity:

Craft a visually consistent identity. This includes your logo, color palette, typography, and overall design aesthetics that resonate with your brand's character.

Crafting a Compelling Brand Story:

Humans connect through stories. Develop a narrative that narrates your shop's origin, journey, and the passion driving your creations.

Consistent Messaging:

Maintain a consistent tone and messaging across all touchpoints—product descriptions, social media, customer interactions—to reinforce your brand voice.

Quality and Value Proposition:

A strong brand stands for quality and value. Consistently deliver products that align with your brand promise to build trust and loyalty.

Visual Consistency in Listings:

Your product images should reflect your brand's aesthetics. Maintain a consistent style, lighting, and background to create a unified visual experience.

Effective Customer Engagement:

Engage with customers authentically. Respond promptly to inquiries, reviews, and feedback to foster a positive brand perception.

Branding in Packaging:

Extend your brand presence to packaging. Thoughtful packaging with branded elements enhances the unboxing experience and leaves a lasting impression.

Leveraging Social Media:

Social media is a dynamic platform for brand engagement. Share behind-the-scenes glimpses, customer stories, and content that aligns with your brand values.

Consistency in Social Media:

Maintain a cohesive visual and messaging style across social media channels. This consistency reinforces your brand's recognition and impact.

Customer Testimonials and Reviews:

Encourage satisfied customers to share their experiences. Positive testimonials and reviews build social proof and enhance your brand's credibility.

Building Community:

Create a community around your brand. Foster interactions, host giveaways, or collaborate with influencers to deepen customer engagement.

Evolving Brand Strategy:

Your brand presence isn't static. Regularly assess market trends, customer feedback, and your brand's performance to adapt and evolve your strategy.

Building a strong brand presence is a meticulous journey of alignment, consistency, and customer-centricity. By crafting a brand identity that resonates deeply with your audience and infusing it into every facet of your shop, you're not just selling products—you're creating an emotional connection that extends beyond transactions. Remember, a strong brand presence is an ongoing commitment, a promise you uphold with every interaction and product, guiding your Etsy venture toward lasting impact and recognition in the marketplace.

Creating a Consistent Brand Identity: A Pillar of Etsy Success

A consistent brand identity is the heart of a successful Etsy shop, communicating your uniqueness, values, and offerings to your audience. Here's a comprehensive guide on how to craft and maintain a consistent brand identity:

Define Your Brand

Core Values and Mission: Clearly articulate your brand's core values and mission. This forms the foundation of your identity.

Unique Selling Points: Identify what sets your shop apart from competitors. Include these distinctive features in your branding.

Visual Coherence

Color Palette: Choose a cohesive color palette that resonates with your brand's personality and appeals to your target audience.

Typography: Select fonts that align with your brand's tone. Consistency in font usage maintains a polished appearance.

Logo Design: Design a memorable logo that encapsulates your brand's essence. Ensure it's versatile and easily recognizable.

Reflect in Product Imagery

Consistent Style: Maintain a consistent style in your product photography. This could include backgrounds, lighting, and angles.

Visual Themes: Incorporate visual themes that align with your brand. For example, if your brand is rustic, use props and settings that convey this.

Uniform Listing Descriptions

Brand Voice: Develop a consistent brand voice for

your product descriptions. This tone could be informative, playful, or elegant, depending on your brand identity.

Storytelling: Weave your brand story into your product descriptions. Customers connect more deeply when they understand the story behind your shop.

Coherent Packaging

Branded Packaging: Extend your brand identity to your packaging materials. Custom stickers, thank-you notes, or branded tissue paper enhance the unboxing experience.

Consistent Design Elements: Ensure that packaging aligns with your color palette, typography, and overall aesthetic.

Social Media Alignment

Visual Consistency: Maintain visual consistency across your social media profiles. Your followers should instantly recognize your content.

Unified Messaging: Share content that aligns with your brand values and resonates with your target audience's interests.

Customer Engagement

Responsive Communication: Respond to customer inquiries and feedback in a manner that aligns with your brand's tone.

Personalized Interactions: Engage authentically with customers, addressing them by name and maintaining a friendly, approachable demeanor.

Feedback Incorporation

Customer Insights: Consider customer feedback when refining your brand identity. Adapt based on their preferences and suggestions.

Continuous Evolution: Brand identity isn't static. It can evolve while still staying true to the core values that define your shop.

A consistent brand identity is your shop's signature, conveying trustworthiness and familiarity to your customers. By aligning visual elements, messaging, and customer interactions with your brand's essence, you're cultivating a strong presence that resonates, builds loyalty, and sets your Etsy shop apart in the competitive marketplace.

Expanding Product Range and Diversification: Elevating Your Etsy Shop

Expanding your product range and diversifying offerings can breathe new life into your Etsy venture. Here's a succinct guide to successfully broaden your horizons:

Market Research: Identify trends and gaps in your niche. Research what customers are seeking to inform your new product additions.

Complementary Products: Introduce products that complement your existing offerings. This encourages cross-selling and appeals to a broader audience.

Quality Assurance: Maintain the quality that defines your brand. New products should meet the same standards that customers associate with your shop.

Customer Insights: Seek feedback from loyal customers. Their preferences can guide your expansion, ensuring you cater to their needs.

Gradual Rollout: Introduce new products gradually. This allows you to monitor their reception and make adjustments as needed.

Consistent Branding: Maintain consistent branding across new and existing products. Visual coherence reinforces your shop's identity.

Market Testing: Experiment with limited releases or prototypes. Market testing gauges demand and helps refine your product offerings.

Sustainable Growth: Ensure your expansion aligns with your capacity to produce, market, and fulfill orders. Sustainable growth is key.

Communication: Inform your audience about new offerings. Utilize social media, newsletters, and your shop announcement to create anticipation.

Continued Evaluation: Regularly assess the performance of new products. Adapt based on sales data and customer feedback for ongoing success.

By diversifying your product range strategically, you're not only broadening your customer base but also showcasing your versatility and adaptability as an Etsy entrepreneur.

PART X: Scaling Your Etsy Business: A Strategic Guide to Sustainable Growth

Scaling your Etsy business is a pivotal step toward achieving greater success and broader reach. However, this journey requires careful planning, resource allocation, and a clear understanding of your market. This comprehensive guide navigates you through the process of scaling your Etsy venture while maintaining quality, customer satisfaction, and long-term sustainability.

Preliminary Assessment:

Before scaling, evaluate your shop's readiness. Assess your existing processes, resources, and market demand to identify opportunities and potential challenges.

Strategic Planning:

Craft a detailed scaling plan. Outline your goals, target market expansion, product diversification, and marketing strategies to guide your growth journey.

Infrastructure Investment:

Ensure your infrastructure can support increased demand. This includes your production capacity, inventory management, and order fulfillment processes.

Quality Assurance:

Maintain the quality that defines your brand. As you scale, prioritize consistent quality in both products and customer service to retain customer trust.

Resource Allocation:

Allocate resources strategically. Consider additional staff, equipment, or technology needed to meet higher demand without compromising quality.

Financial Planning:

Create a financial plan that accounts for increased expenses and potential fluctuations. Secure adequate funding to support your scaling efforts.

Market Research:

Continuously research your market to identify evolving trends and customer preferences. Adapt your product offerings and strategies accordingly.

Marketing Expansion:

Extend your marketing efforts to reach new audiences. Utilize social media, collaborations, and advertising to increase your brand's visibility.

Streamlined Operations:

Optimize your processes for efficiency. Automate repetitive tasks, refine workflows, and eliminate bottlenecks to accommodate higher order volumes.

Scalable Technology:

Utilize technology to streamline operations. E-commerce platforms, inventory management software, and customer relationship management tools can enhance efficiency.

Customer Engagement:

Maintain personalized customer engagement. As your customer base grows, retain a genuine connection through responsive communication.

Employee Training:

If you're expanding your team, invest in training. Ensure your employees understand your brand values, processes, and customer service standards.

Test and Iterate:

As you scale, test new strategies in controlled environments. Analyze results and iterate based on data to refine your approach.

Sustainability Focus:

Sustainable growth considers long-term viability. Avoid rapid expansion that could strain resources and impact your shop's reputation.

Continuous Adaptation:

Scaling isn't a one-time effort. Adapt to changing market dynamics, customer feedback, and industry trends to remain relevant.

Scaling your Etsy business demands a holistic approach that aligns growth with customer satisfaction and brand integrity. By strategically expanding, maintaining quality, and embracing continuous improvement, you're navigating the path toward sustainable success. Remember, the journey of scaling is ongoing; as you conquer new milestones, you're shaping your Etsy venture into a thriving, resilient, and impactful presence in the marketplace.

Strategies for Scaling Production and Sales

Scaling your Etsy business requires a balanced approach to both production and sales. Here's a concise guide to effectively scale these critical components:

Efficient Production Scaling:

Streamline Processes:Analyze your production workflow and identify inefficiencies. Streamline processes to increase output without compromising quality.

Batch Production: Batch similar tasks or products to optimize time and resources. This minimizes setup and transition periods.

Automation Integration:

Where feasible, integrate automation tools or machinery to expedite production and reduce manual labor.

Quality Control:

Maintaining quality is non-negotiable. Implement rigorous quality control measures to ensure consistent standards as production scales.

Supplier Partnerships:

Forge strong partnerships with suppliers. Negotiate favorable terms and ensure a steady flow of raw materials.

Inventory Management: Optimize inventory levels to avoid stockouts or excess. Real-time inventory tracking prevents disruptions in sales.

Evolving Sales Strategies:

Diversified Offerings: Introduce complementary products to expand your offerings and attract a wider customer base.

Bundling and Packages: Create product bundles or packages to encourage larger purchases and cross-selling opportunities.

Strategic Pricing: Adjust pricing based on increased production costs and perceived value, ensuring profitability amid higher demand.

Sales Channels Expansion:

Multiple Platforms: Explore selling on multiple platforms to diversify revenue streams and reach a broader audience.

Wholesale Opportunities: Consider entering the wholesale market to supply retailers, opening doors to bulk orders and increased exposure.

Collaborations: Partner with other brands or creators for collaborations that expand your reach and introduce your products to new audiences.

Marketing and Promotion:

Targeted Advertising: Invest in targeted advertising to increase visibility among your ideal customer base.

Content Marketing: Share valuable content related to your niche. Blog posts, videos, or social media content can attract and engage potential customers.

Social Media Engagement: Amplify your presence on social media platforms through regular posts, stories, and engagement with your audience.

Customer Engagement:

Personalized Communication: Maintain personalized interactions with customers. A genuine connection fosters loyalty and word-of-mouth referrals.

Customer Feedback: Listen to customer feedback and adapt based on their preferences. This indicates your dedication to their happiness.

Scalable Technology:

E-commerce Platforms: Utilize scalable e-commerce platforms that accommodate increased traffic and sales.

Order Management Systems: Implement order management systems to efficiently handle larger order volumes.

As you navigate the journey of scaling production and sales, remember that maintaining the delicate balance between quality, efficiency, and customer satisfaction is paramount. Embrace adaptable strategies that enable sustainable growth and allow you to capitalize on the expanding opportunities in the Etsy marketplace.

Outsourcing and Delegating Effectively

As your Etsy business grows, effectively outsourcing and delegating tasks can help you focus on strategic aspects while ensuring operational efficiency. Here's a concise guide to make outsourcing and delegation work for your venture:

Assess Your Needs:
Identify Repetitive Tasks: Pinpoint tasks that are time-consuming but don't require your direct involvement.

Evaluate Core Functions: Determine tasks that are central to your expertise and brand, which you should retain control over.

Select the Right Tasks:

Non-Core Activities: Outsource or delegate tasks that aren't directly tied to your creative process or brand identity.

Skill-Based Tasks: Delegate tasks that require specialized skills or expertise that you don't possess.

Choose the Right Partner:

Vendors and Freelancers: Select reliable vendors or freelancers with a track record of quality work and timely delivery.

Virtual Assistants: Hire virtual assistants for administrative tasks, customer support, or social media management.

Clear Communication:

Detailed Briefs: Provide clear instructions and expectations to your outsourced partners. A detailed brief reduces the chances of misunderstandings.

Regular Check-Ins: Maintain open communication with your team to address questions, provide feedback, and ensure alignment.

Quality Control:

Sample Tasks: Start with small tasks or projects to gauge

the outsourced partner's quality and reliability

Feedback Loop:Establish a feedback loop to ensure tasks meet your standards and make necessary adjustments if needed.

Cost-Effectiveness:

Cost-Benefit Analysis: Consider the cost of outsourcing against the time saved and the potential revenue generated.

Long-Term Value: Evaluate the long-term benefits of outsourcing, such as freeing up your time for revenue-generating activities.

Gradual Delegation:

Start Small: Begin by outsourcing one or two tasks before gradually expanding to more complex responsibilities.

Build Trust: As you gain confidence in your outsourced partners, delegate more critical tasks.

Monitoring and Evaluation:

Performance Metrics: Set performance metrics and evaluate the effectiveness of outsourcing efforts regularly.

Flexibility: Be open to adjusting your outsourcing strategy based on performance and evolving business needs.

Outsourcing and delegating effectively can unlock your potential to focus on growth strategies, product innovation, and customer engagement. By leveraging specialized skills and external support, you're optimizing your time and resources to elevate your Etsy venture to new heights.

PART XI: Adapting to Change and Trends

In the dynamic landscape of Etsy, the ability to adapt to change and embrace evolving trends is a fundamental skill for success. As market preferences shift and new opportunities arise, staying relevant and agile is key. This comprehensive guide navigates you through the art of embracing change and riding the waves of trends in the Etsy marketplace.

Recognizing the Need for Adaptation:

Market Dynamics: Be attuned to shifts in customer preferences, buying behaviors, and emerging market trends.

Competitor Analysis: Study your competitors to identify their strategies, strengths, and weaknesses. Adapt based on these insights.

Embracing Trendspotting:

Market Research: Dedicate time to continuous market research. Identify trends in product design, color schemes, and consumer demands.

Customer Insights: Engage with your customers to understand their changing needs and preferences. Their feedback is a valuable source of trend information.

Staying Ahead of the Curve:

Early Adoption: Don't hesitate to embrace emerging trends. Being an early adopter can position your shop as a trendsetter.

Creativity: Infuse your unique creativity into trends. Adapt them to match your brand's identity while remaining appealing to your target audience.

Balancing Innovation and Brand Identity:

Maintaining Core Values: While embracing trends, ensure they align with your brand's core values and mission.

Innovation Within Niche: Innovate within your niche. Reinterpret trends to create unique products that cater to your specific audience.

Flexibility in Product Offerings:

Expand or Adjust: Adapt your product range to incorporate trending items or variations that resonate with current consumer demands.

Limited-Edition Releases: Utilize limited-edition releases to test the waters for new trends before committing to full-scale production.

Visual Identity Evolution:

Update Visuals: As trends shift, consider updating your branding elements, such as logo, color palette, and product photography, to maintain a modern appeal.

Consistency Amid Change: While evolving, maintain visual consistency across your shop's branding to retain recognition.

Marketing Agility:

Content Strategy: Tailor your content strategy to incorporate trending keywords, hashtags, and topics to enhance discoverability.

Social Media Adaptation: Pivot your social media content to reflect current trends, showcasing your shop's relevance.

Feedback Loop:

Customer Feedback: Listen to customer feedback on new products or adaptations. Adjust based on their responses.

Iterative Improvement: Use feedback as a guide for iterative improvements, ensuring your shop aligns with evolving customer preferences.

Monitoring Performance:

Data Analysis: Regularly analyze sales data, traffic sources, and customer interactions to identify trends and assess their impact.

Sales and Profitability: Evaluate whether trends lead to increased sales and profitability. Balance creative expression with financial viability.

Embracing change and trends is a dynamic dance that keeps your Etsy venture relevant and resilient. By harnessing the power of innovation, customer insights, and a keen eye for emerging market dynamics, you're setting the stage for continuous growth and success amidst the ever-evolving Etsy marketplace.

Staying Informed about Etsy Updates and Flexibility in Response to Market Trends

Staying ahead in the fast-paced world of Etsy requires a twofold approach: staying informed about Etsy updates and maintaining flexibility to respond to evolving market trends. Here's how to move across this dynamic environment:

Stay Informed about Etsy Updates

Etsy Seller Updates: Regularly review Etsy's official seller updates and announcements. These provide insights into policy changes, new features, and improvements to the platform.

Newsletters and Blogs: Subscribe to Etsy's newsletters and official blogs. These sources often share tips, success stories, and guidance on adapting to platform changes.

Community Participation: Engage in Etsy's community forums and groups. Sellers often share their experiences, insights, and updates related to the platform.

Flexibility in Response to Market Trends

Continuous Trendspotting: Keep an eye on changing consumer preferences and market trends. Leverage social media, industry publications, and market research to stay updated.

Adaptation Strategy: Build flexibility into your business strategy. Be prepared to adjust your product offerings, marketing tactics, and branding in response to emerging trends.

Quick Iterations: Incorporate new trends swiftly. From product design to marketing campaigns, prioritize agility in your approach to align with current market demands.

Feedback Utilization

Customer Feedback: Listen to customer feedback about your products and shop. Adapt your offerings based on their suggestions and preferences.

Sales Data Analysis: Regularly analyze sales data to identify which products are resonating with customers and which may need adjustment.

Balancing Brand Identity and Trends

Brand Consistency: While embracing trends, ensure they align with your brand's core values and visual identity.

Unique Interpretation:Incorporate trends in a way that's unique to your brand. Infuse your signature style into trending elements.

Testing and Learning:

Trial Runs: Test new products or adaptations on a small scale before committing to a full launch. This minimizes risk while gauging customer interest.

Iterative Approach: Learn from trial results and customer feedback. Iterate and refine your approach to effectively leverage trends.

Staying informed and flexible positions your Etsy venture for success. By combining a keen awareness of Etsy updates, a finger on the pulse of market trends, and a willingness to adapt, you're fostering resilience and relevance in an ever-changing marketplace.

PART XII:Reflecting and Looking Forward

As an Etsy entrepreneur, the journey is characterized by continuous growth, learning, and evolution. Reflecting on past achievements and challenges while setting your sights on future aspirations is a critical process that propels your venture forward. This comprehensive guide explores the significance of reflection and foresight in your Etsy journey.

The Power of Reflection

Celebrate Milestones:Take a moment to celebrate your achievements. Think back on your progress and how far you've come.

Learning from Challenges: Consider the challenges you've faced. Reflect on what you've learned from them and how they've contributed to your growth.

Analyzing Successes

Identify Winning Strategies: Reflect on what strategies led to your successes. Isolate the factors that contributed to positive outcomes.

Replicate Success: Identify if there are successful approaches that can be replicated in other aspects of your shop's operations.

Assessing Opportunities for Improvement

Areas of Growth: Reflect on areas that require improvement. Identify aspects of your shop, products, or processes that could be refined.

Customer Feedback: Review customer feedback to pinpoint recurring suggestions or issues. Increase client happiness by using this information.

Setting New Goals

Long-Term Vision: Reflect on your long-term vision for your Etsy venture. How has it evolved, and what steps are needed to get closer to that vision?

SMART Goals: Set specific, measurable, achievable, relevant, and time-bound (SMART) goals for the coming months or year.

Foresight and Planning

Market Trends: Anticipate upcoming market trends and shifts. Research and adapt your offerings and strategies accordingly.

Innovative Ideas: Reflect on innovative ideas that align with your brand. How can you introduce new, unique products or approaches?

Balancing Reflection and Action

Actionable Insights: Ensure your reflections translate into actionable insights. Identify tangible steps you can take based on your reflections.

Course Correction: Reflecting also allows you to course-correct if you've strayed from your original vision or goals.

Creating a Feedback Loop

Regular Review: Set aside time regularly to review your shop's progress, strategies, and goals.

Iterative Improvement: Use your reflections to iteratively improve your shop's operations and offerings.

Fostering Adaptability

Lessons from Reflection: Reflecting on past adaptability and innovation can inspire you to remain flexible and open to change.

Market Dynamics: Consider how your shop can stay resilient and relevant in the face of changing market dynamics.

The journey of an Etsy entrepreneur is an ongoing cycle of reflection, learning, and growth. By harnessing the insights gained from reflecting on your journey thus far and strategically planning for the future, you're cultivating a mindset of continuous improvement and evolution that will propel your Etsy venture toward even greater heights of success.

Celebrating Milestones and Achievements: Marking Your Etsy Journey

In the dynamic world of Etsy entrepreneurship, celebrating milestones and achievements is essential for acknowledging your progress and motivating further growth. Here's a concise guide to embracing these moments of success:

Acknowledge Progress

Reflect on Journey:Take a moment to reflect on your journey so far. Consider where you started and how much you've achieved.

Small Wins Matter: Celebrate not only big milestones but also the smaller victories that contribute to your overall progress.

Motivation Boost

Renewed Energy: Celebrating achievements rejuvenates your spirit, energizing you to tackle new challenges with enthusiasm.

Positive Reinforcement: Recognition reinforces your commitment and hard work, reinforcing a positive mindset.

Rewarding Efforts

Personal Gratification: Celebrating milestones is an opportunity for personal gratification, reminding you of the value you bring to your Etsy venture.

Self-Care: Treating yourself to something special or indulging in a well-deserved break is a way to recharge and refresh.

Inspiration for Growth

Setting New Goals: Celebrations often inspire you to set higher goals and chase even loftier aspirations.

Embracing Challenges: The feeling of accomplishment gained from celebrating milestones can embolden you to face new challenges with confidence.

Sharing Success

Community Engagement: Sharing your achievements within the Etsy community fosters connections and allows you to inspire others.

Customer Engagement: Celebrate milestones with your customers as a way to thank them for their support and loyalty.

Fostering Gratitude

Grateful Mindset: Celebrating milestones cultivates gratitude, grounding you in the present and reminding you of the journey's significance.

Team Recognition: If you have a team or partners, celebrating milestones acknowledges their contributions as well.

Reflecting on Growth

Measuring Progress: Milestones offer tangible markers for measuring how far you've come and how much you've learned.

Adaptable Mindset: Reflect on the strategies that led to success and consider how they can be adapted for future growth.

Cultivating Positivity

Positive Vibes: Celebrating achievements injects positivity into your Etsy journey, creating an atmosphere of excitement and optimism.

Resilience Reminder: Recognizing what you've overcome reminds you of your resilience and ability to navigate challenges.

Celebrating milestones and achievements isn't just about the present—it's an investment in your future success. By acknowledging your progress, fostering positivity, and using these moments as stepping stones toward new endeavors, you're nurturing a mindset of continuous growth and excellence in your Etsy entrepreneurship journey.

Embracing Continuous Learning and Growth

In the ever-evolving landscape of Etsy entrepreneurship, the pursuit of continuous learning and growth is paramount. Here's a succinct guide to how embracing a mindset of ongoing improvement can elevate your Etsy journey:

Embrace Curiosity

Stay Inquisitive: Maintain a curious mindset, always seeking to understand new trends,technologies, and customer preferences.

Open to Exploration: Be open to exploring unfamiliar territory, whether it's a new product category or a fresh marketing strategy.

Learning from Challenges

Turning Obstacles into Lessons: View challenges as opportunities to learn. Each setback can provide valuable insights for improvement.

Adapt and Overcome: Use lessons from past challenges to adapt your strategies and overcome future hurdles.

Seeking New Knowledge

Industry Insights: Stay updated on industry trends, both within your niche and in the broader e-commerce landscape.

Skill Enhancement: Continuously refine your skills, whether it's product design, customer service, or marketing tactics.

Feedback Utilization

Customer Feedback: Value customer feedback as a source of insights. Use it to improve the overall consumer experience as well as your products and services.

Iterative Improvement: Iterate based on feedback to create products and interactions that resonate with your audience.

Adapting to Change

Market Dynamics: Recognize that change is constant. Adapt your strategies to stay relevant in the face of shifting market trends.

Innovation Mindset: Embrace innovation, introducing new products or approaches that reflect changing customer preferences.

Self-Reflection

Analyzing Progress: Regularly reflect on your journey's evolution. Recognize your areas for improvement and honor your achievements.

Mindful Adjustments: Use self-reflection to make mindful adjustments to your business strategies and personal development.

Investing in Education

Courses and Workshops: Consider taking relevant courses or attending workshops to enhance your skills and knowledge.

Networking: Engage with fellow entrepreneurs, attending events or online forums to exchange ideas and gain insights.

Fostering Resilience

Overcoming Setbacks: View setbacks as learning opportunities rather than failures. This mindset fosters resilience and adaptability.

Positive Response: Respond positively to challenges, embracing them as chances to strengthen your entrepreneurial skills.

Goals and Aspirations

Setting Ambitious Goals: Continuously set ambitious yet achievable goals that motivate you to strive for excellence.

Growth Mindset: Maintain a growth-oriented perspective that sees setbacks as part of the journey toward success.

Embracing continuous learning and growth is a commitment to your personal and professional development. By staying curious, adapting to change, and learning from every experience, you're forging a path of excellence in your Etsy entrepreneurship journey that's marked by innovation, resilience, and unwavering determination.